THE **BIG BOOK** OF
**AUTOCORRECT**
**FAILS**

Published in 2014 by Prion
An imprint of Carlton Books Limited
20 Mortimer Street
London W1T 3JW

Copyright © 2014 Carlton Books Limited

A CIP catalogue record for this book is available from the British
Library.

ISBN 978-1-85375-920-8

Printed in the UK by CPI Group (UK) Ltd, Croydon, CR0 4YY

# THE BIG BOOK OF AUTOCORRECT FAILS

## TIM DEDOPULOS

PRION

# Introduction

In these days of superfast digital communication, never has the phrase "shoot the messenger" been more relatable to so many people, all over the world. No sooner had the predictive text feature been added to most smartphones around 2007 than the hilarious global phenomenon of "autocorrect errors" boomed too. In the time it takes to press SEND, the entire world went from being obsessed with sending messages to being obsessed about the alarming errors that can occur *when messaging*. And for good reason too.

Just like to calling your history teacher "mom" every day, sending embarrassing messages has become just another one of life's ritual humiliations. But, unlike calling your history teacher "mom" – which is *your* fault – when it comes to a message sent in error, you should always blame your phone's stupid autocorrect feature.

In fact, by the time you've finished reading this sentence, tens of million messages will have been sent, many of them, no doubt, in error and with some truly outstanding autocorrect results. And that's where we come in.

The mammoth tome you are holding in your hands is the best of those brilliant mess-ups; a truly bonkers collection of some of the world's greatest examples of messaging meltdowns and autocorrect bungles, belly-flops and fails – all caused by momentary lapses in attention, drunkenness and your so-called 'smart' phone!

Read each entry carefully, study them and make sure you don't suffer the same misfortunes other poor souls have. And, for goodness' sake, be especially careful when using the words duck, aunt, election and tentacles.

YOU HAVE BEEN WARNED.

Enjoy!

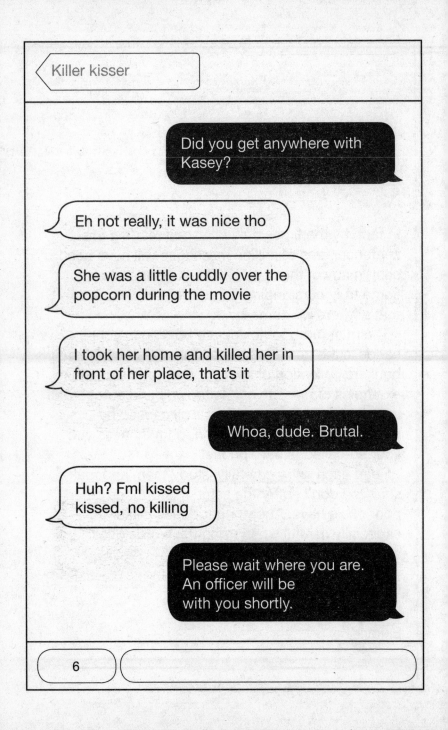

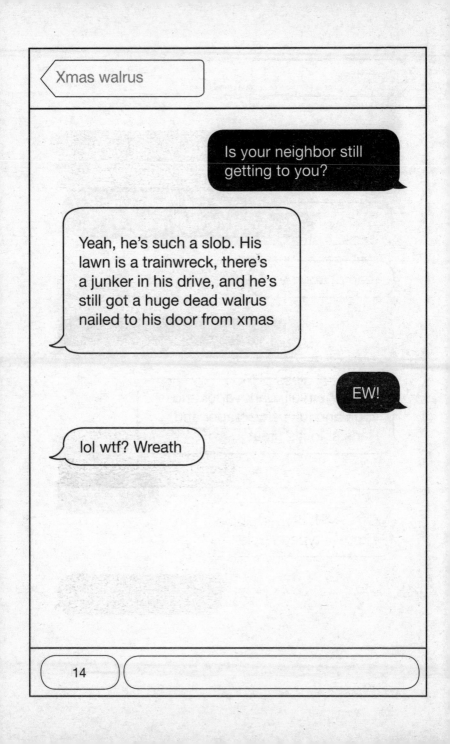

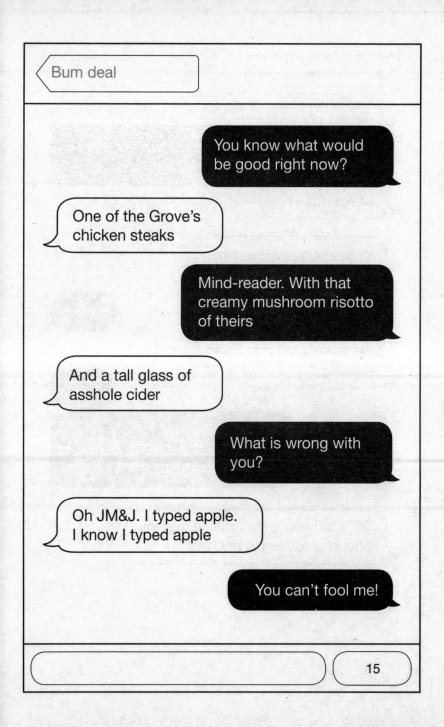

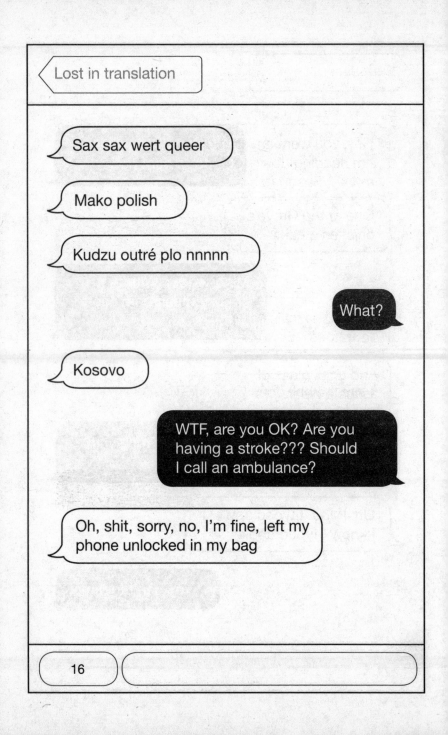

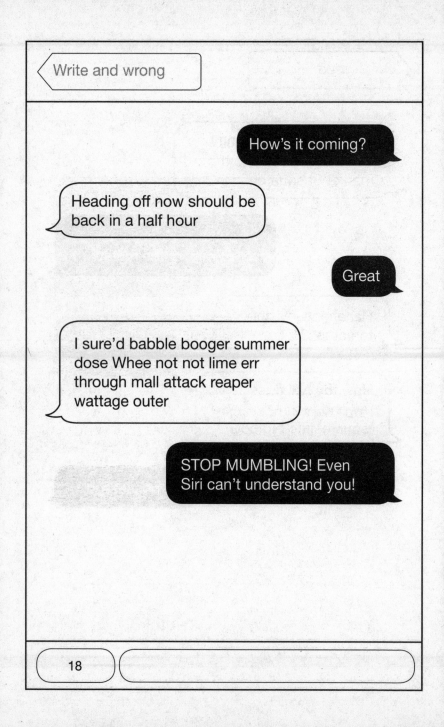

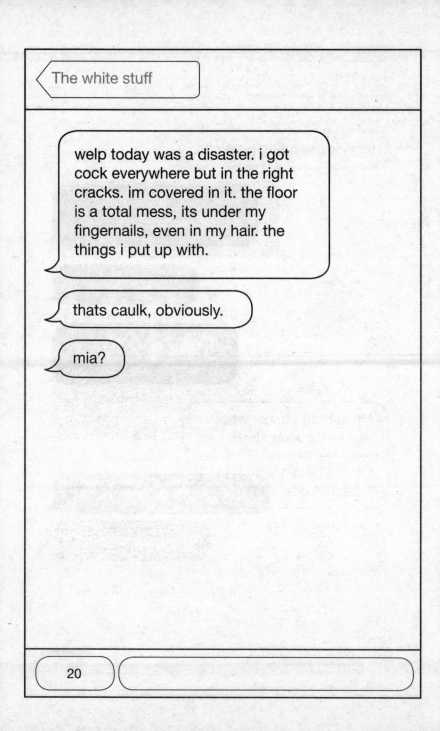

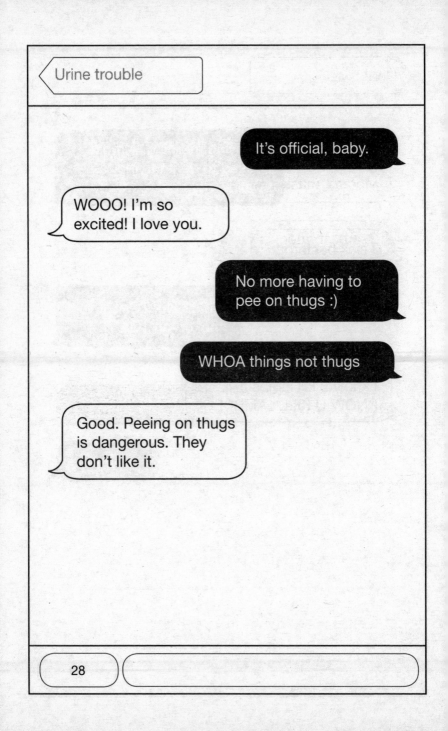

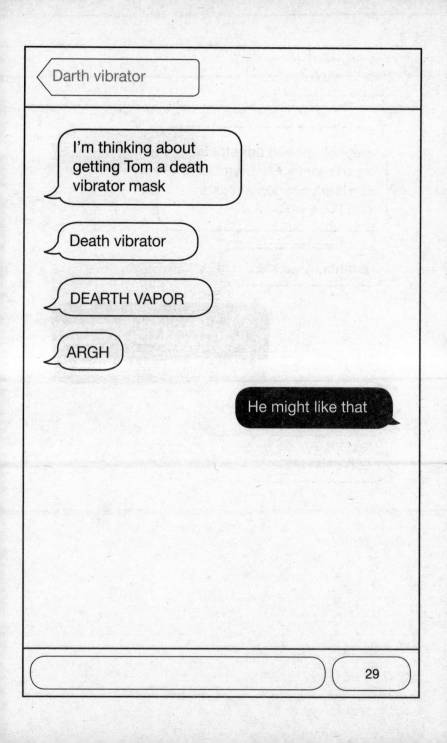

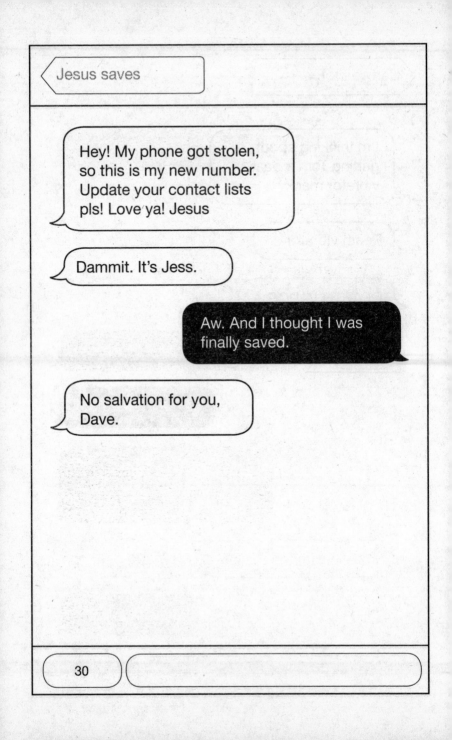

How did it go?

She wasn't convinced. She didn't like the drapes.

That's inconvenient. What was wrong with them?

I think it's threshold Gerry thing shellfish like.

Uh...

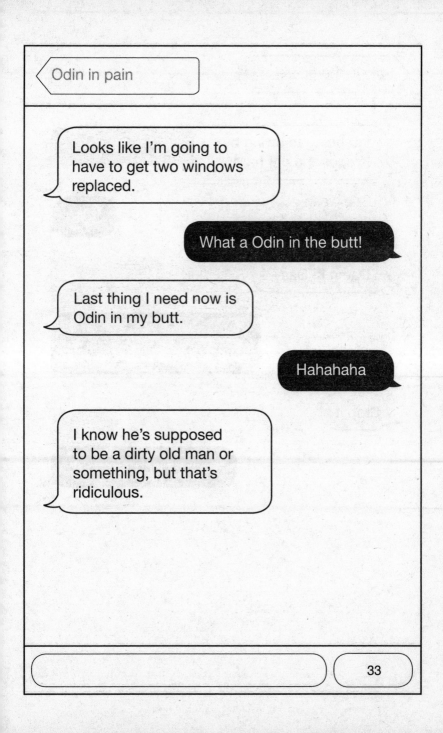

I'm going to get to practice around 7, grab a wrap afterwards, then go curl up on the couch with Dexter and a big glass of wine.

Lucky you. I'm going to be fondling landlady.

Wow. I don't know what to say.

What? Oh, this horrible brick. Folding laundry.

Sounds much less exciting.

Yeah. Also much less gay. And my landlady is an old, chunky, Polish guy called Vlad.

Hey, can you help me with a tech question?

I can try.

What sort of lead do I have to use to plug my camera into my cooter?

Are you OK?

I don't know. It was terrible. I feel like I died a bit.

I'm sorry, hun. I'll give you a big cuddle to bang you back from the dead.

Wow, inappropriate much? Bring.

At least you got me to laugh!

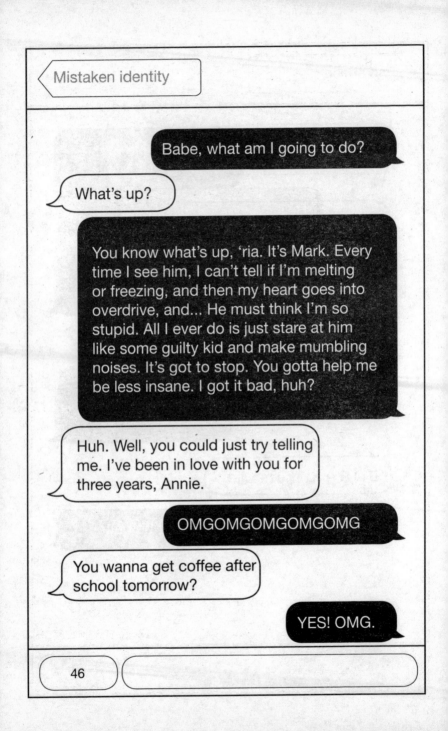

You going to watch the match at Ed's?

Nope. I'm just going to grab a beer, shit in my chair and unwind.

What, you're john's busted again?

Crap.

Think you got enough of that already!

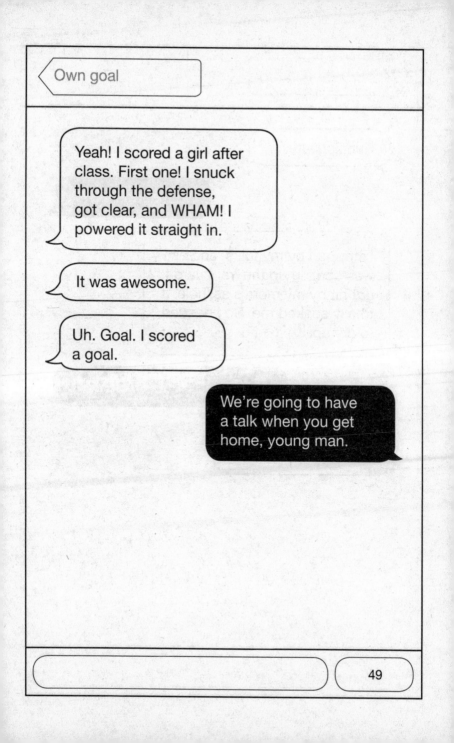

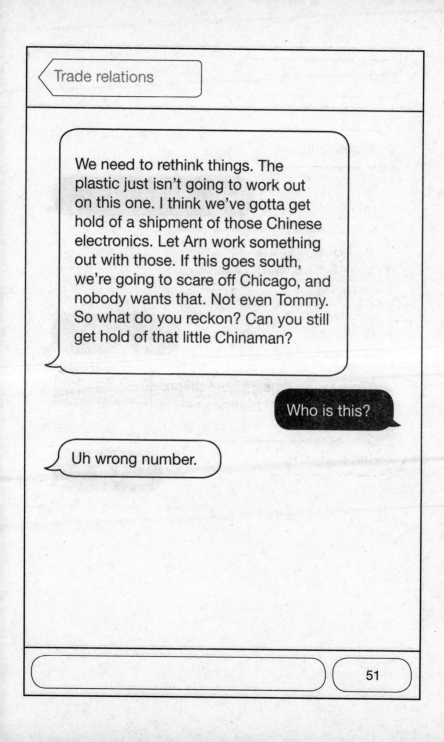

We need to rethink things. The plastic just isn't going to work out on this one. I think we've gotta get hold of a shipment of those Chinese electronics. Let Arn work something out with those. If this goes south, we're going to scare off Chicago, and nobody wants that. Not even Tommy. So what do you reckon? Can you still get hold of that little Chinaman?

Who is this?

Uh wrong number.

Are you OK?

NO.

How about if I came over with Krispy Koreans?

\* \*

Right. Krispy Kremes.

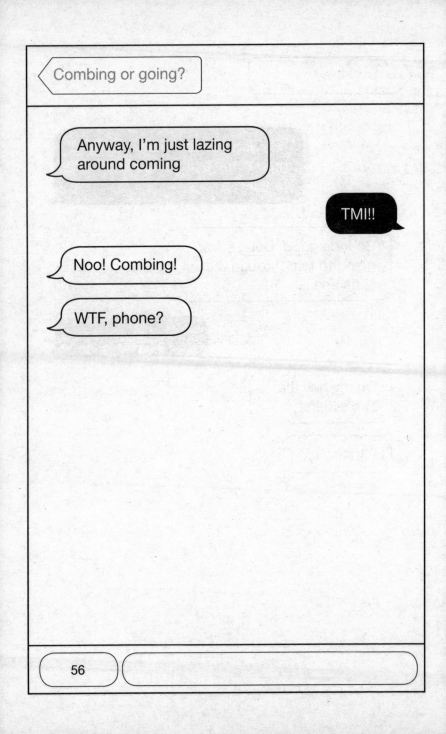

I'm heading in to town. I've got to pick up some of Rod's shits from the cleaner.

HAHAHAHAHAHA

Lol yeah, we get all are best turds laundered regularly.

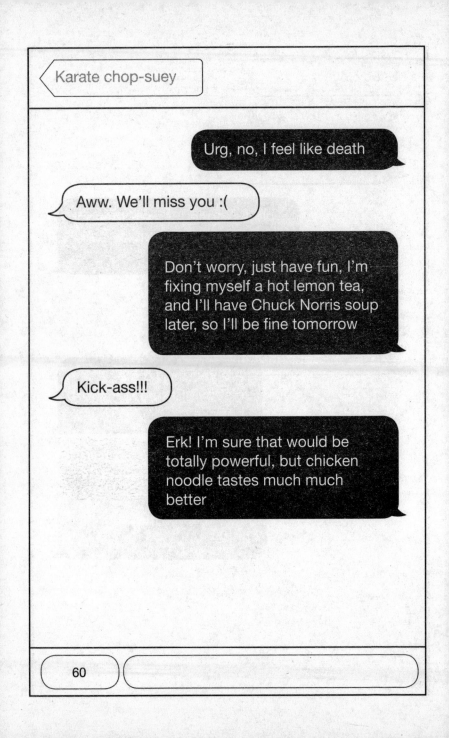

OMG did you see that ep of game of throbs?

What the heck have you been watching?

Hahahahahahahaha

A song of Ass and foreplay!

Truth

Not too bad. We had about four inches of rice and the pond flooded the back yard, but no serious damage.

Whoa

WTH? Rain. No rice fell from the sky.

What about frogs?

Plenty of frogs. None from the sky.

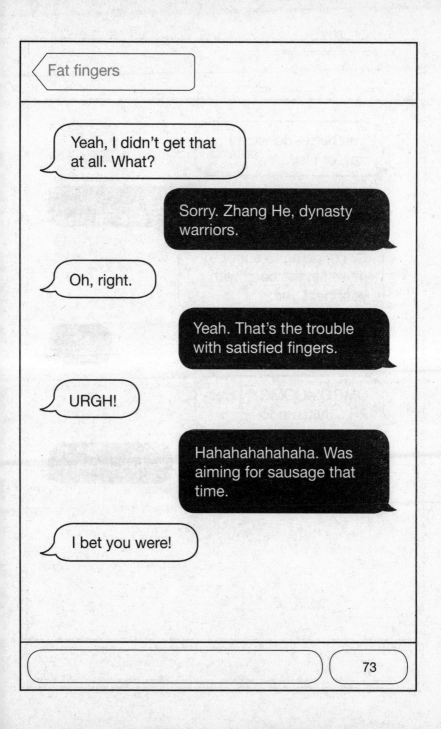

Doing some last-minute pick-ups. Anything you'd like in your stalking?

Hmm. Let's see. A hot vacuum flask of coffee is always good. Some donuts, maybe. Good binoculars. A list of local ladies who forget to pull the curtains. Oh, yeah, probably some sort of night vision video camera thing too. And one of those big sports holdalls so I can pretend I'm just coming back from the gym if anyone sees me.

Ha! You have all that already!

Sleep well, my dead.

Yeah, right, that'll give me sweet dreams.

Hahahahaha. Dear. Hope you're not dead.

Not yet. I don't like the look of the doll in the corner though

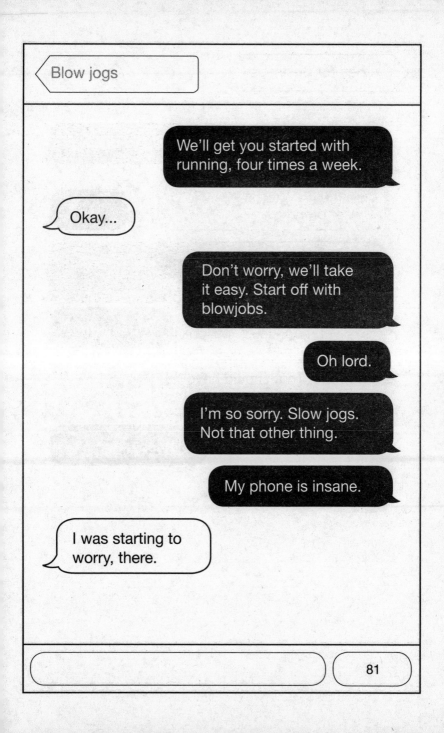

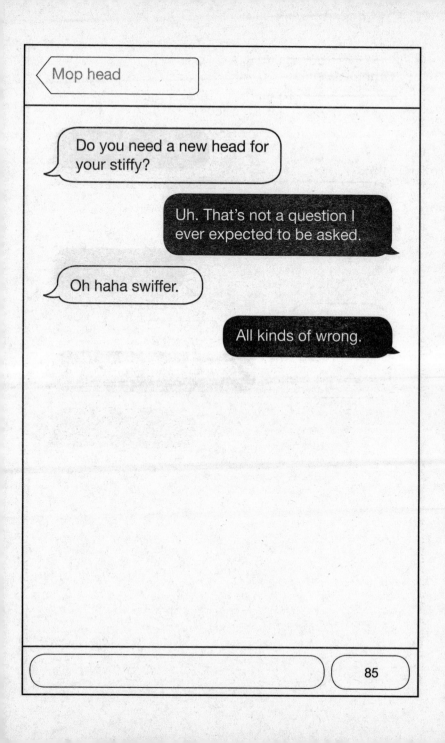

Oral fixation

Miss you, babe

Aww. You always know how to make me smoke.

I do? Shee-it.

Smile lol

ROFL right back at ya

Did you hear about that cat cafe?

No?

You can go in there and get a coffee and they have lots of cats in there to keep you company

Too cute!!!! I've got to go. I haven't been able to punch a cat in forever!

>_< WHAT?

OMG! TOUCH. Why would I punch a cat?

Cos you're evil. EEEVIL. But they'd call the cops on you if you tried it.

Come on over. Girls' night. We'll get some Chinese, open a bottle of wine, and watch a good child fuck. It'll be a blast.

Nnng.

Chick flick.

God, I hope the NSA aren't reading this.

You're on the list now...

89

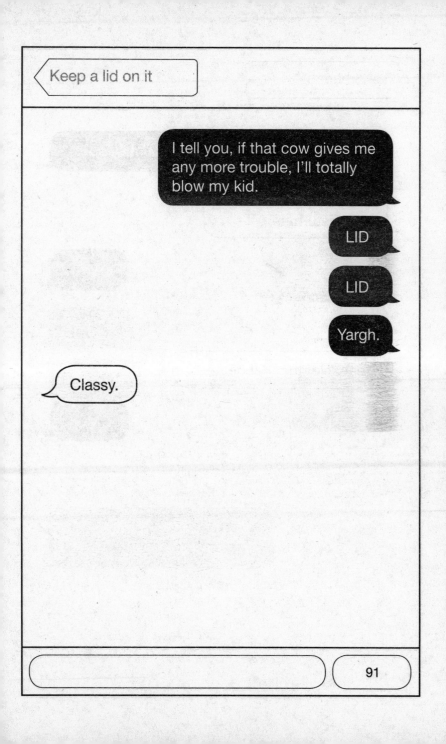

Ugggghhhhh cant sleep

U shld do what I do an masturbate

OMG

............

Yeah. Not that. Meditate

OMG

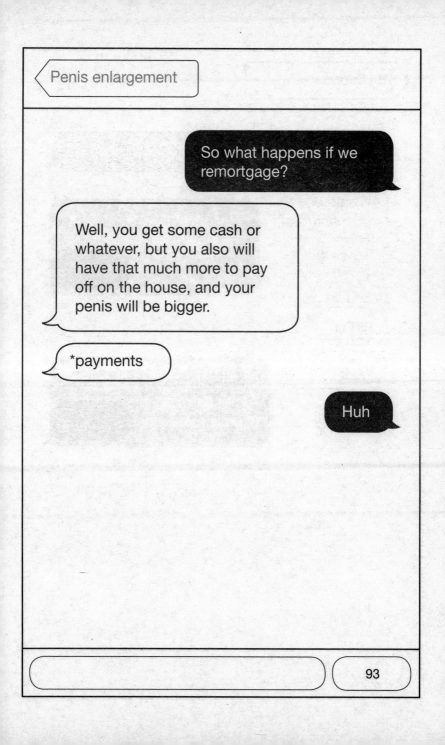

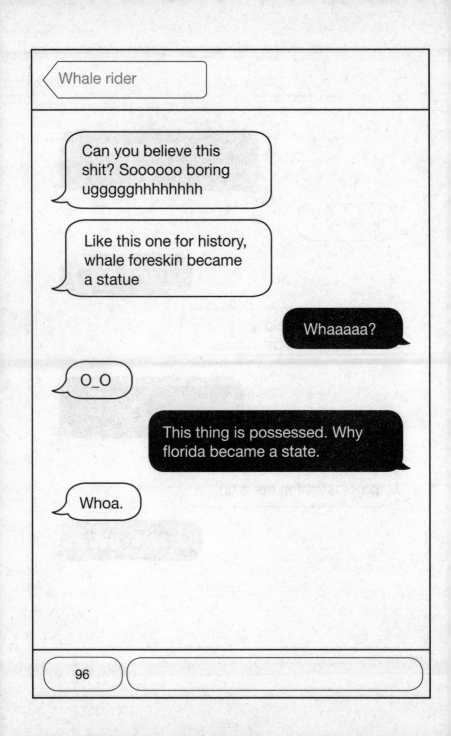

I'm cooking on Sunday. I'm really looking forward to some juicy dick.

You go, girl!

*dies*. I'm cooking a duck.

Hahahahaha

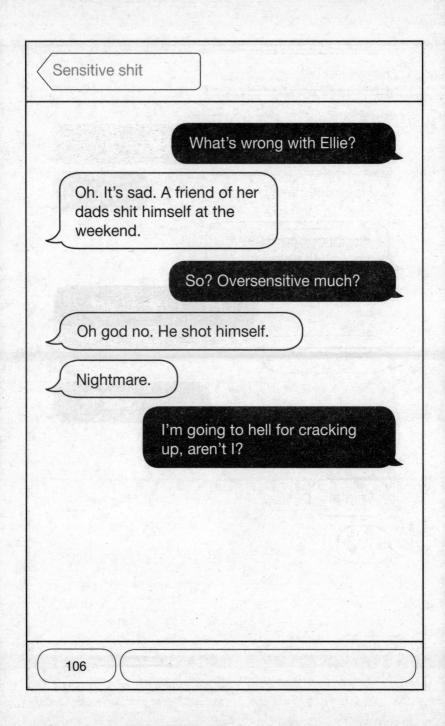

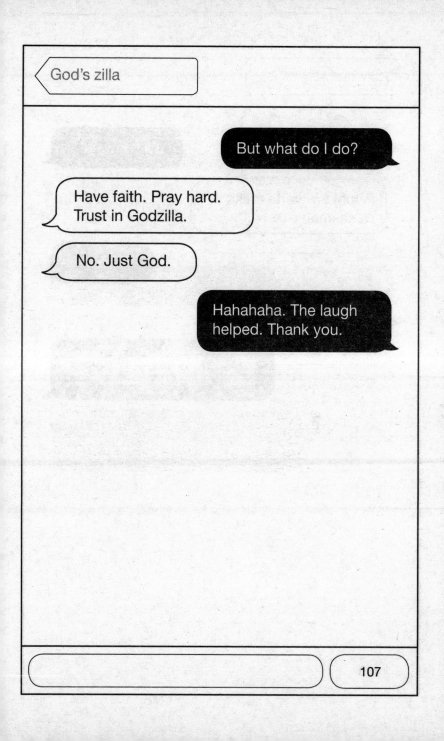

It's snowing!

Woo! We gotta make a sexman

A what?

sexman haha

Oh no, now I imagined it and it won't go away

S'up, Lily?

Do you want to teach me to drink? Don't tell my Dad tho.

Whoa. Sure thing! How's tomorrow night?

Whoa there, boy. Stupid autocorrect. Drive, not drink.

Damn.

You wish!

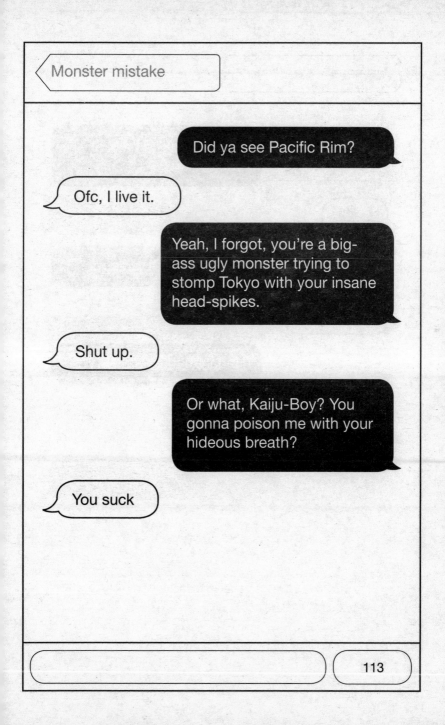

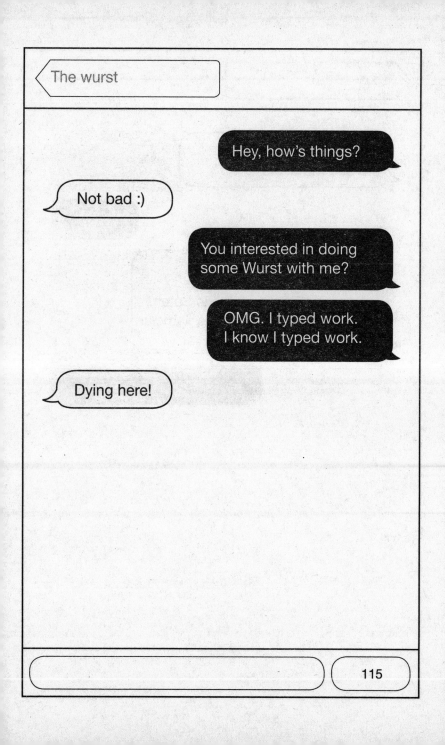

Fancy a dump later?

Huh. Not that it's any of your business, but no, I'm good for the day thanks.

Oh ugh. That should be drink.

Hahahahaha. I thought you were turning German on me.

Sure, sounds good.

Ugh. Annoying day. Got held up in meetings, and now I've got to make an appointment to go see the fucktard.

Uh, you mean your boss?

OMG. No, the doctor. How did that happen? My doctor is a decent guy!

Bad day. My condom engine blew up.

Uh, how does that even work?

It's like a steam engine, but you run it on condoms instead of water.

Just feed 'em in and whoosh, off it goes.

What? Really?

Of course not really, dumb ass. CAR ENGINE!

Totally. Last thing I need now is to get dick.

Hahahahahahaha.

Not sure you're right about that, sweetie.

OMGOMGOMGOMGOMG

*sick

Too late!

Skate mate

Skates?

Oh yeah, totally. I love ice-mating.

No.

;-) I bet

Skating, dammit.

It's so cute! Izzy is in the nativity play, and they've given her a little costume and everything. She's the Christmas fart!

Oh! That should be fart

This wretched phone. f a i r y.

Poor Izzy!! LOL

Are you on it?

Yeah, I'll send a massage to her.

Do you really think that's necessary?

Uh, maybe not. I might make do with just a message.

No happy endings on the company dime!

I thought I might go hit up some nature at Tampon Bay

Ewwwwwwww

Just gross

LOL LOL LOL OMG Tarpon!!

My lord.

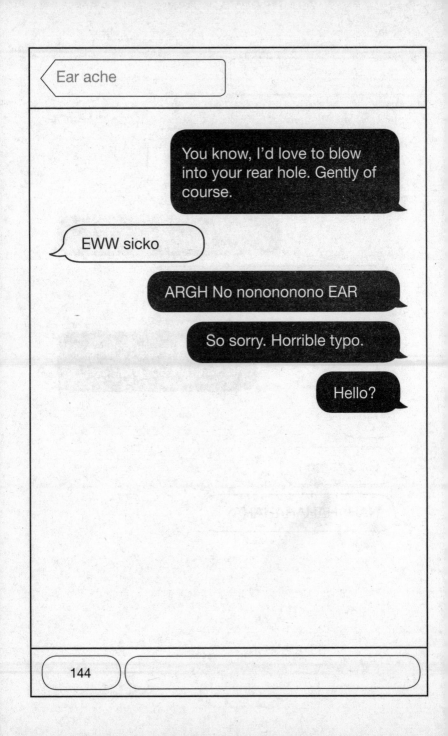

Dirty socks

You down Dennys?

Soon

Trying to find a pair of clean cocks

Whoa sorry I asked

I can't breathe

Must be those cocks!!!

socks socks socks

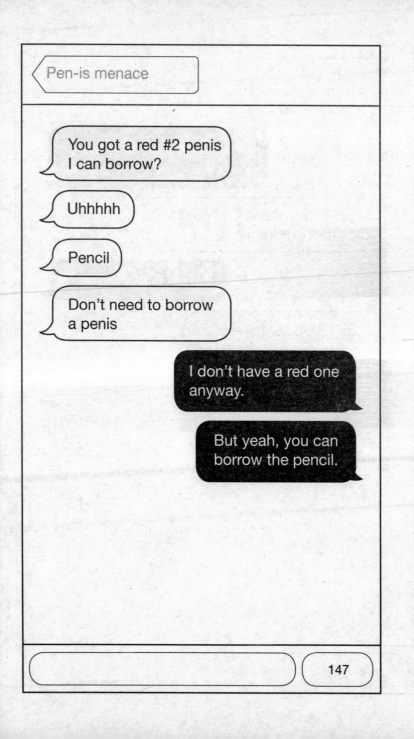

How are you holding up, lovie?

Urgh. Been better. Still getting dick every morning.

Wow. Lucky Brady!

I can't stop laughing!!!!

I don't think a vomiting wife is much of a turn-on!

Goodnight love.

Night. Wish I was there to run my tigers through your hair.

Mmm. Hair tigers.

Hunting the wild jungles of my head.

Feeding on the brain-monkeys.

Loon!! (*fingers)

I guessed! Night x

I'm heading out for a wad

The hell does that mean? Sounds disgusting. Or sick.

LOL. Walk.

Still sounds disgusting!

Miss you xxx

Miss you too. I'm cuddled up with one of your shits so I can smell you.

Gods alive, there's an image.

Nooooooooooo!!!

I really hope you meant shirt :)

I did! I totally did!

ROFL

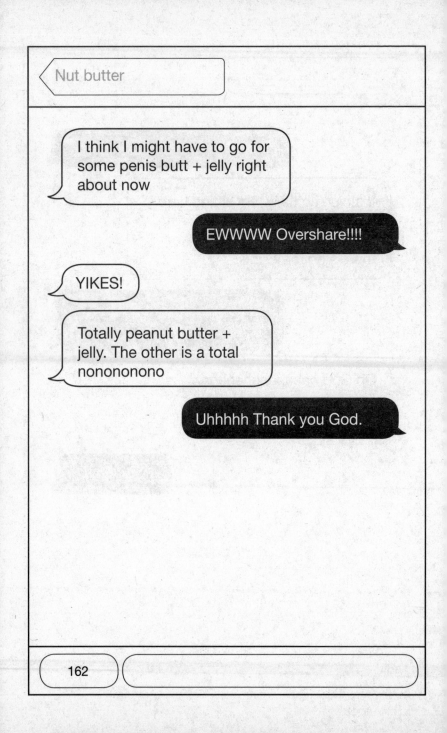

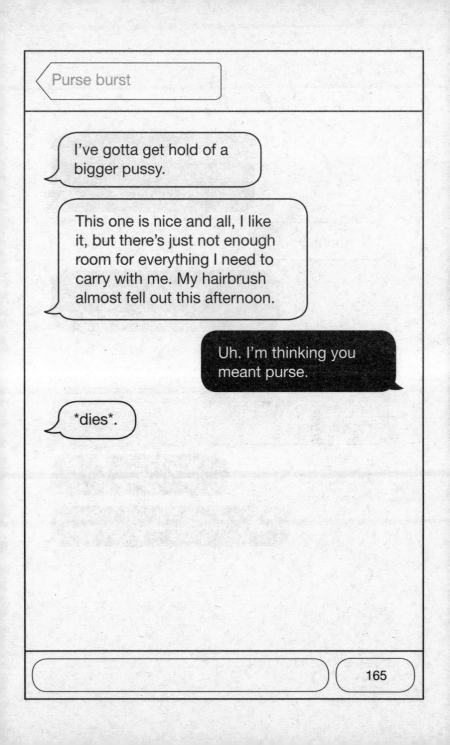

I should be out real soon now. Homo from hot lips at last!

Christ on a cracker. HOME FROM HOSPITAL.

Sounds like you're out all ready, 'hot lips.'

Ha ha very ha

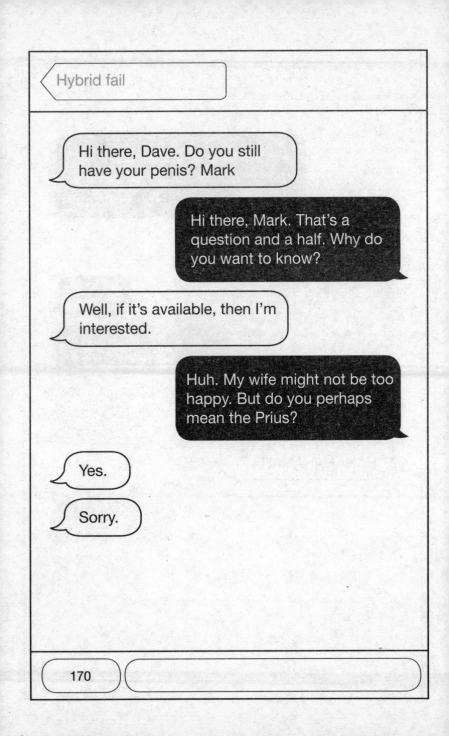

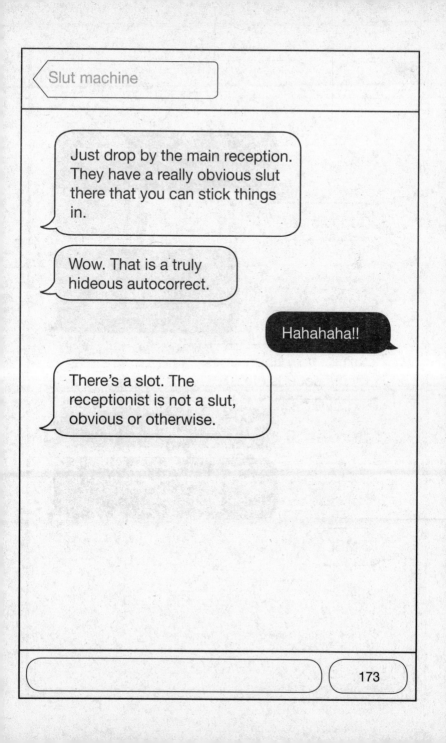

I'll be getting into town around 7.45p. If the bus is going to be late, I'll drop you a text.

Kk. I'll make sure there's a taco waiting for you.

Gee, thanks.

LOL! Don't worry, I'll include a newspaper you can use as a blanket.

You're all heart.

You want a big piece of card and a marker pen? Or just the *TAXI?

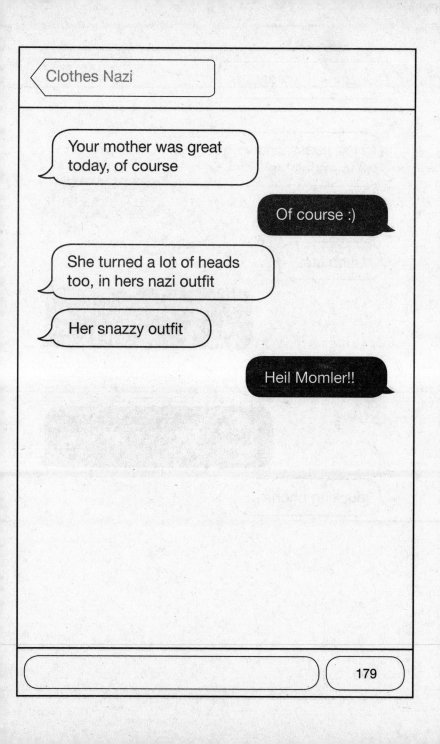

You ever try cameltoe tea? So relaxing.

What the hel is wrong with you?

Crap on a stick. * chamomile. Little flowers.

Nasty.

Wash your mouth out

How bout you?

Yeah, not much. Just washing the dick.

Ah crap.

Dishes.

Yeah, TMI! LOL

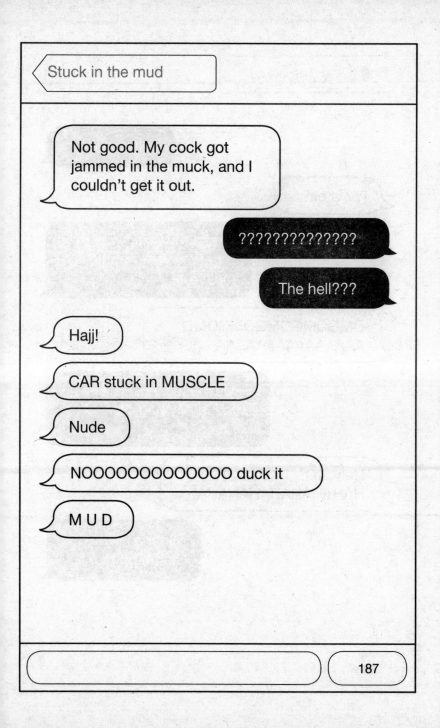

You wouldn't harken to have a 13x9" baking pan with high sides that I could borrow, would you?

Yea, verily do I say that such wondrous treasure is indeed within mine compass, so be ye not wroth, but hasten thy homely posterior to mine humble abode wherein the prize does rest, that thou mayst claim in for thine own purposes, for a time.

Hey! Watch whose butt you're calling homely!

And thanks :D

Front door's locked.

Go in the sith door. That's open.

Go in the sith door. That's open.

Dude, I can't do that.

Why not?

Still Light-Side.

OMG Hahahahahahahaha

Dude fewd

Hey.

Doodie.

*doodie

OFF

DOODIE

Stop calling me that!

I give up

Bro.

Thanks for a fun afternoon, Matt. We all had a great time. Kira and the kids were really impressed with your magic dick too - you'll have to show us more next time!

Hm. That really didn't sound good, did it?

I meant magic trick, for the record.

I don't know whether to laugh or shriek!

I'm going to be doing a pan of lasagna. Maybe you could bring some Taliban bread?

I'm not sure. Afghanistan is a long way out of my way, y'know? Plus I'm not sure that you really want a loaf that's sworn to kill us infidels. Could be risky.

* Italian

Much safer, yeah. Good idea.

Al said you might know where to source some stage rigging.

Hm. I can't think of anything available before next week. Sorry, dude. I'm not sure what to suggest, other than to wish you luck with your c**t.

Whoa. *HUNT.

Seriously sorry, man.

Yeah, OK. Thx

Not much. Chilling. You?

Getting ready for my grandma's sex teeth.

OMG

Sixtieth. She's 60.

Oh god the images go in but they don't come out

You telling me?
AAAAAAA

I'm seeing it at 3.

Don't forget to check it has arctic condom

Yeah, I'm hoping not seem like a crazy cat lady.

Hahahahahahaha

This phone is insane

Airconditioning

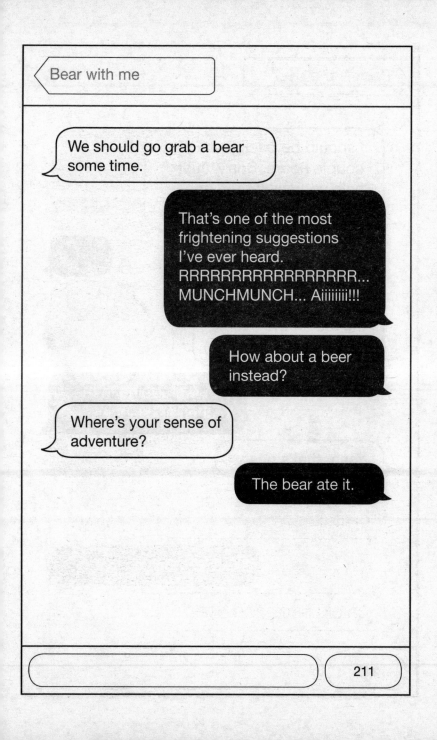

OK, I just puked up outside your place.

WTF? Why are you such a jerk??

*pulled up

Relax, no vomit

Oh. Um, sorry.

:P

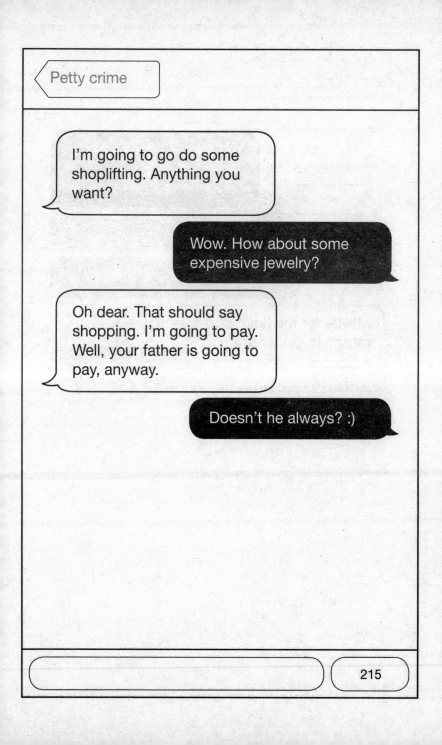

You should have seen Jessica's rectal performance. Beautiful.

Talk about multi-talented.

Oh God hahahahaha *recital

Maybe for the best. She seems a bit shy for anal porn.

XDD

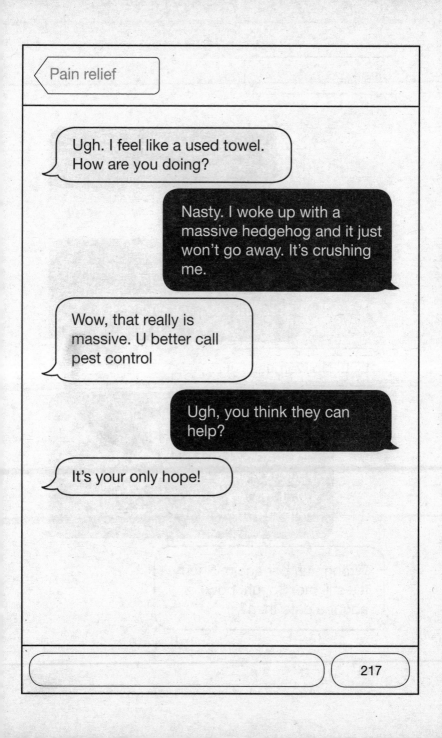

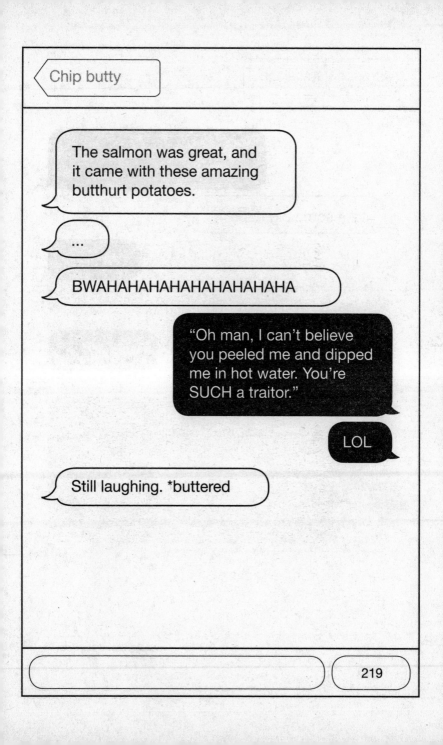

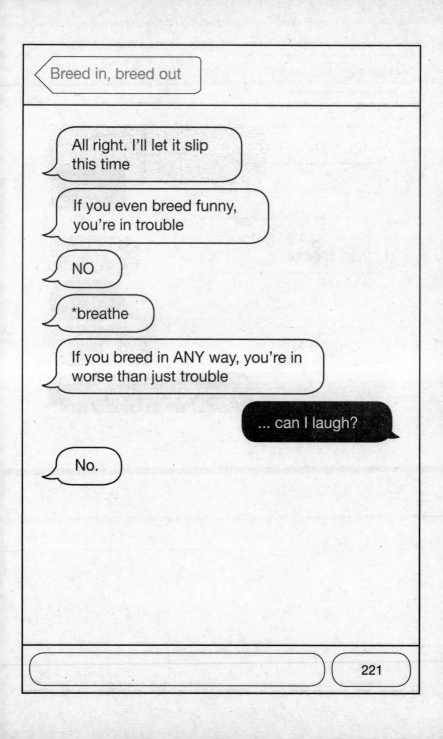

Ugh.

This car is driving me crazy. I gotta go get my tits balanced.

!!!!!!!

FFS! My tires.

Hahahahaha

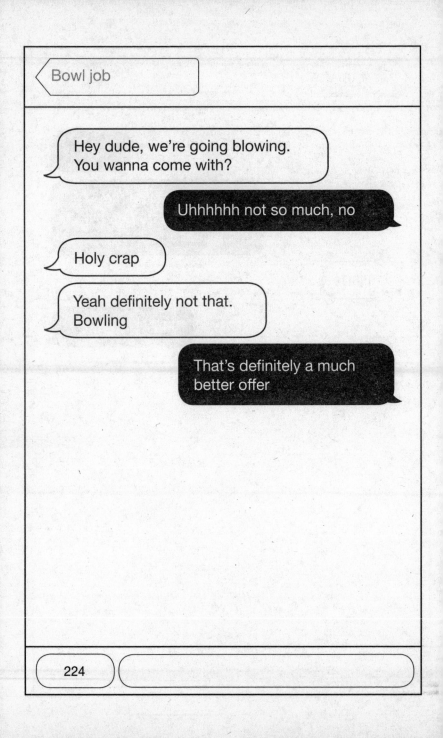

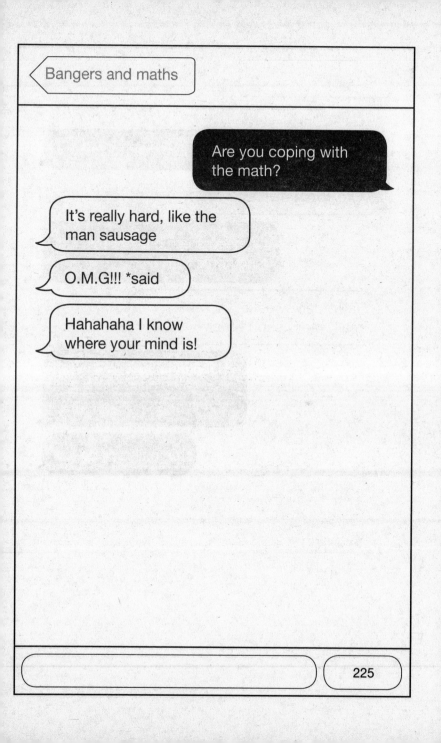

You anywhere near town?

Ofc. What d'ya after?

:) I need some bits of dowel, and some 5" Nazis

Tall order, sweetie. Or, rather, really really short order

Hahahaha Just go down that shitty biker bar with a shrink ray!!

Or nails will do.

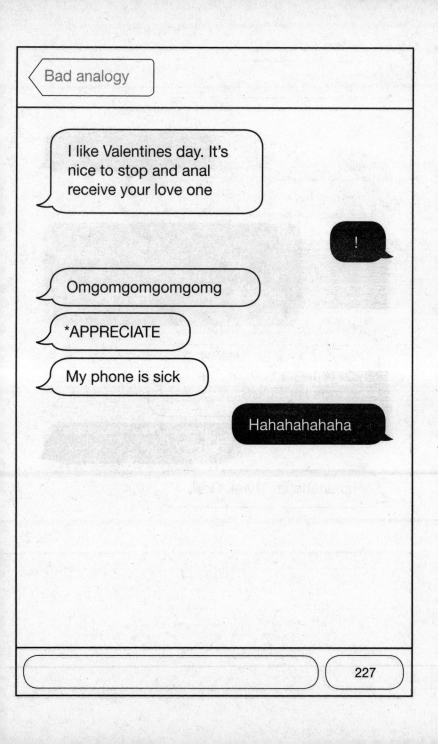

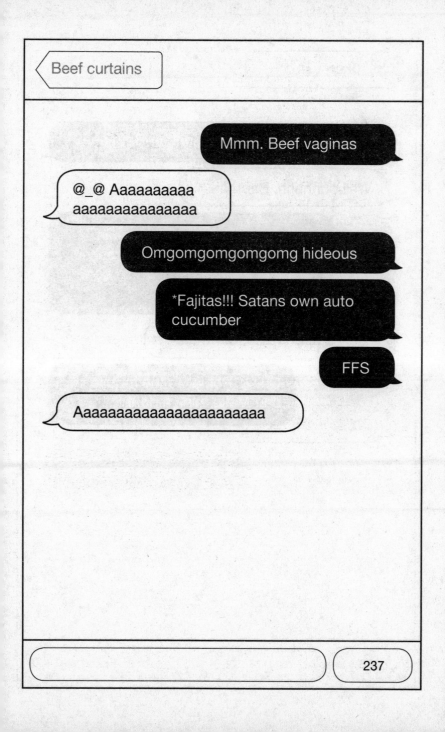

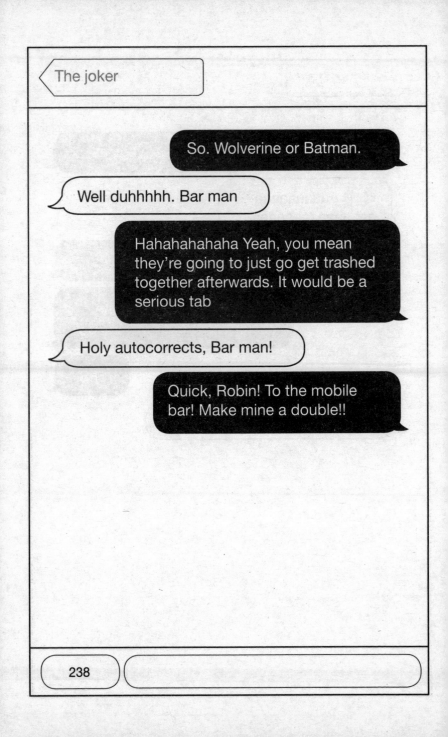

How about if we meet up an hour before?

Sure. It would be nice to catch up a bit. We can have a decent shart

Christ, I hope not!

Hahahaha *chat. I don't know about the other.

Do not look it up. You don't need that in your head!

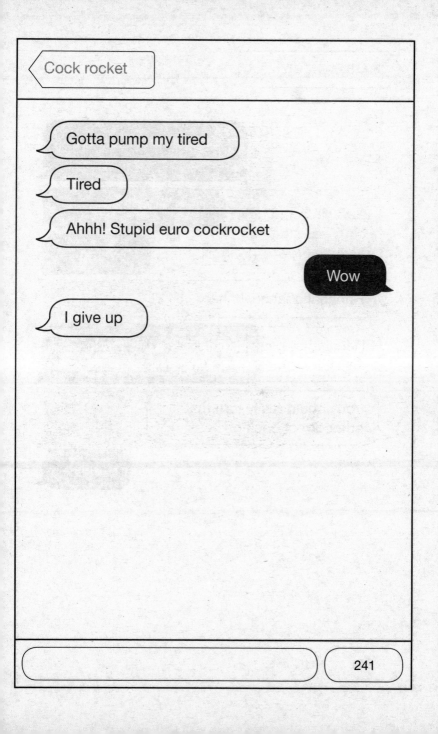

Could you out some beefsteaks for tonight?

I don't know, sounds a bit cruel. I mean, are they ready for it? Maybe they're scared of how their parents are going to react.

You lost me.

It could be they're in the closet for a reason. You ever think about that, huh? I THINK NOT!!!

Or I could just cut your steaks instead.

Ohhhhh Hahahahaha

Hi love. Been to collect the idiots yet?

Sorry, pa. I think you meant to send that to Mom.

Oh yeah, thanks.

HEY! Are you calling us idiots?!

You have to ask?
Like I said...

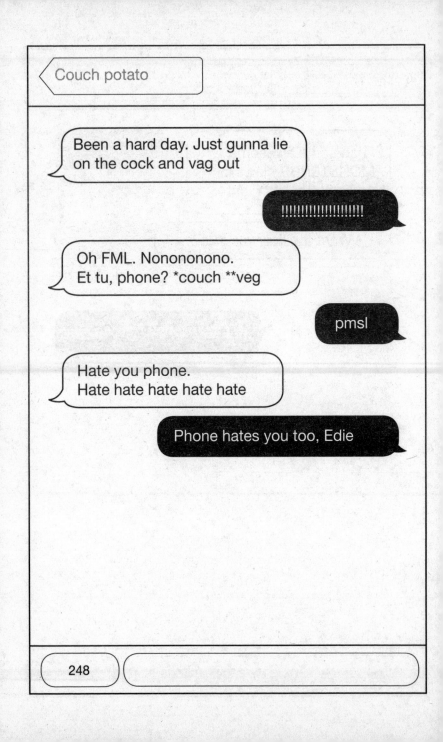

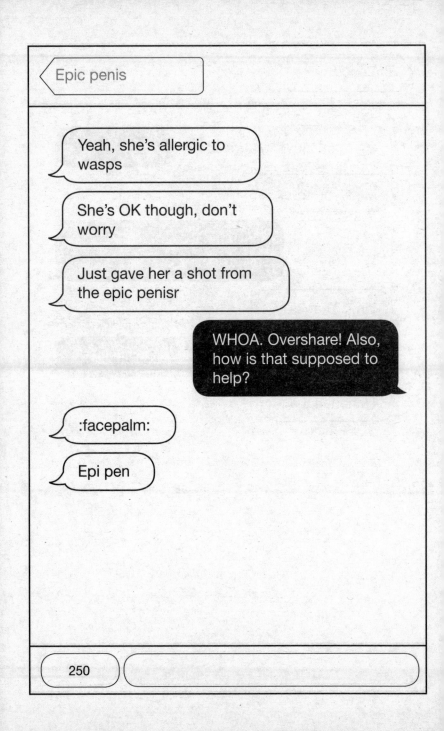

Feel dreadful.

You ok?

Not right now. Mu whole head is stuffed with rum.

?? Alky!

Oh go away. Don't mock the affliction. Flem.

So you're Ok with picking me up?

Sure. Just go wank for me on the corner.

Hell no!!

Definitely not my thing!

*wait

You wait!!

Heck, it's cold. Brrrr. Qubwer is coming.

Oh man, not Qubwer! Beware his frumious snatch and his icy cleats!

New House Stark motto right there. Qubwer is Coming.

Lucky Qubwer!

Is there anything I can do to help?

Well, if you'd pleasure the vacuum around the lounge, that would be a help

...

Oh lord. Not that, I beg you. Just PLEASE RUN it.

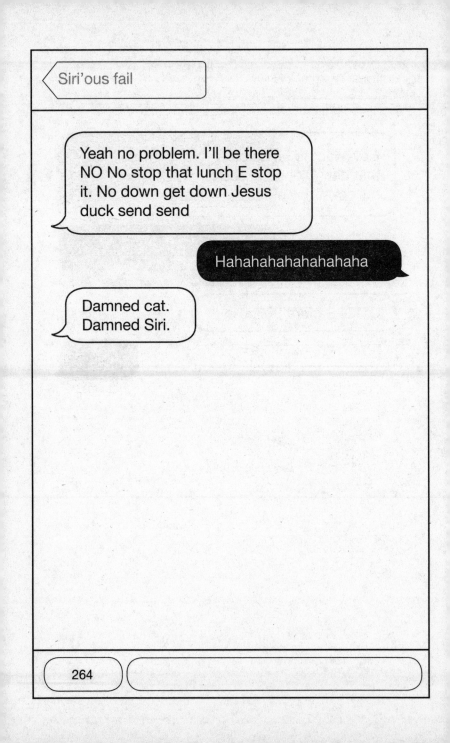

Yeah no problem. I'll be there NO No stop that lunch E stop it. No down get down Jesus duck send send

Hahahahahahahahaha

Damned cat.
Damned Siri.

Just take care, OK?

Of course. I can hear how terrible it is. The ram is really loud on the metal hooves.

Whoa. EPIC.

LOL! Yeah, it's snorting fire out of its nostrils. It must be as tall as a bus. I think it has acid saliva, too.

LOOOOOOOOOOOOOOL

The rain is loud as well, what with the metal roof.

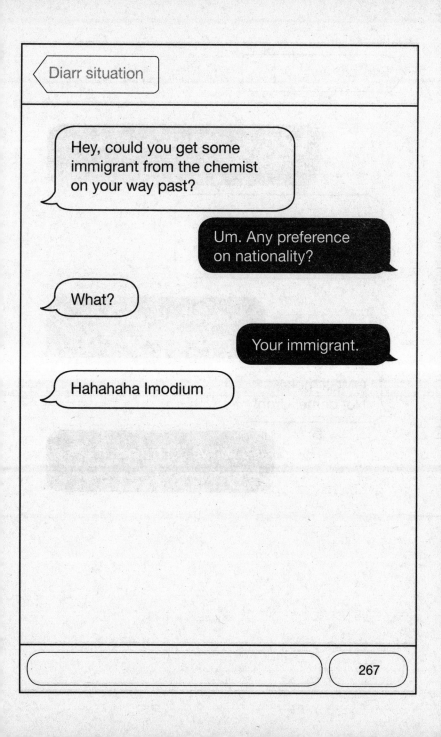

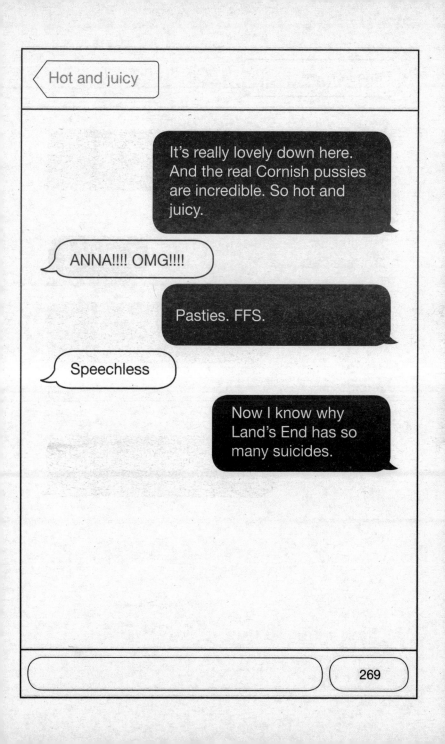

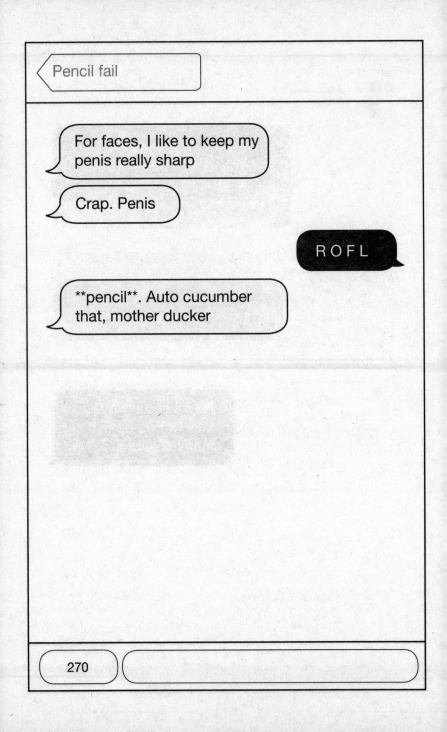

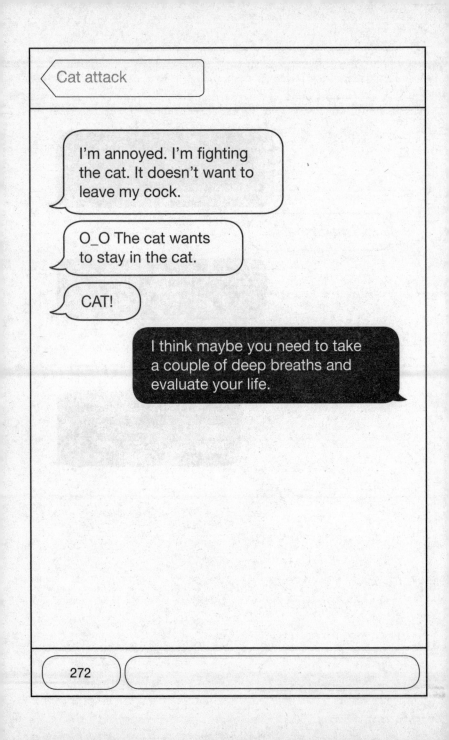

Oh god, they served up these nasty little bits of octopus testicle all chopped up in a red sauce

HOLY CRAP. That's a seriously niche food.

GOD!! That would be even worse. Tentacle was bad enough.

How many octopus would you have to kill to have enough testicles for six people?

... I'm thinking one is still too many

Maxie was running around for hours, and when he finally came back, he was dragging this enormous dick, and he totally refused to put it down or give it to me for like twenty minutes. There's something not right with that dog.

Omg. STICK

LOOOOOOOOO OOOOLLLLLLLL

Takes after his mistress!!

I think she's a window.

Not window, window.

Well, that clears it up.

WINDOW!

You can see right through her?

Her husband died.

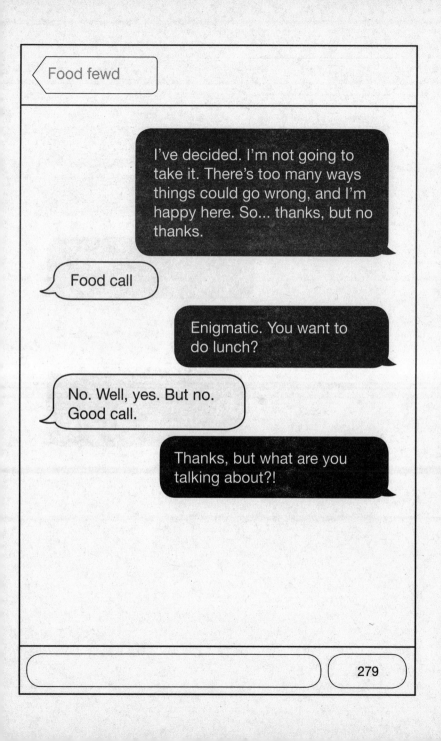

I've decided. I'm not going to take it. There's too many ways things could go wrong, and I'm happy here. So... thanks, but no thanks.

Food call

Enigmatic. You want to do lunch?

No. Well, yes. But no. Good call.

Thanks, but what are you talking about?!

Uhhh so tired. Blue Warrior needs sleep badly. I can hardly do my John today. My boss is not happy.

... By boss, you mean pimp?

WHAT? Urrrh. Not helping. *job

Hahahahaha. You're awesome when you're exhausted.

Yeah, I really like her. I'm grinning like an idiot.

She certainly seems to have made a difference for you.

She's like a breath of fresh ass.

That good, huh???

ROFLLLLLLLLL

*air

What are you getting for dinner? I'm having some meat loaf with mashed parasites.

Oh my god, that's the most disgusting thing I've ever heard!

Ew!

*potatoes

Sick sick SICK!!
I lost my appetite.

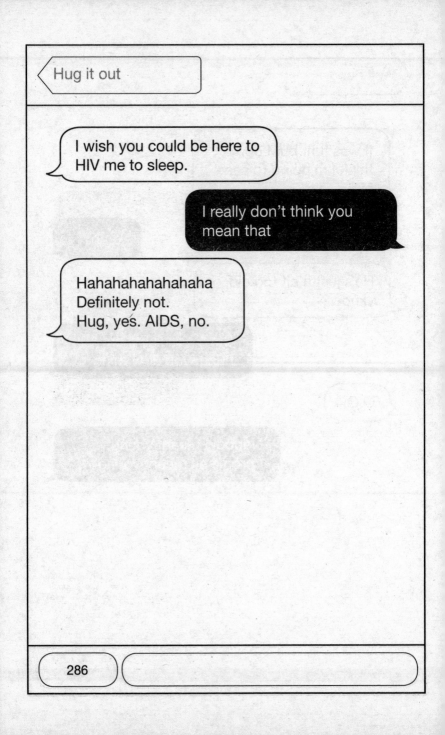

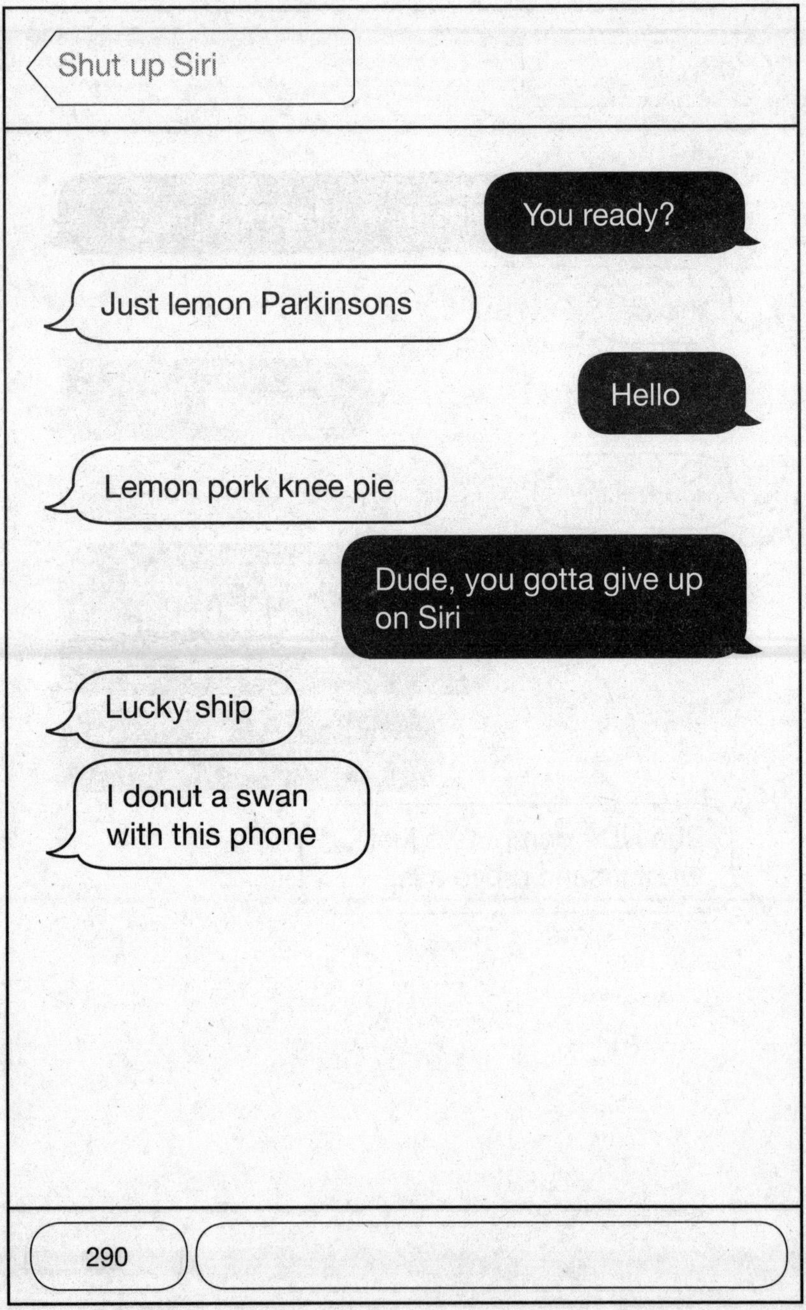
Shut up Siri
You ready?
Just lemon Parkinsons
Hello
Lemon pork knee pie
Dude, you gotta give up on Siri
Lucky ship
I donut a swan with this phone

It's been terrible.

Now we have some guy running around the house fingering every hole in sight. It stinks.

Aaa!!!

Holy shit. FUMIGATING. I...

LOOOOOOOL

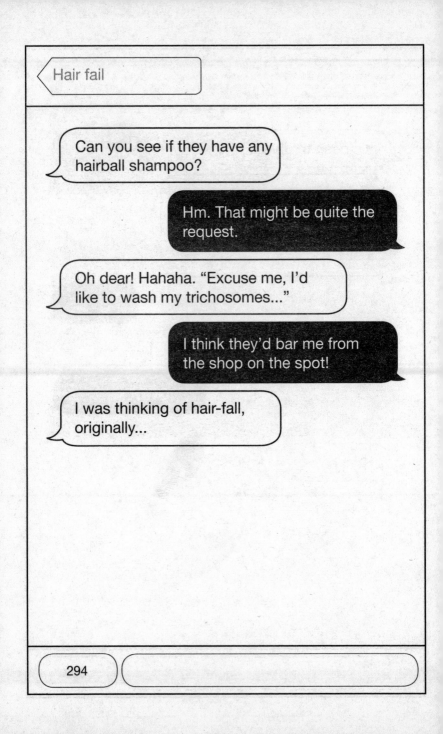

Can you see if they have any hairball shampoo?

Hm. That might be quite the request.

Oh dear! Hahaha. "Excuse me, I'd like to wash my trichosomes..."

I think they'd bar me from the shop on the spot!

I was thinking of hair-fall, originally...

You're my wide

Are you calling me fat LOL?

Hahaha definitely not! I like my nose unbroken :)

Good move :) Your phone better watch it, though!

You out yet, bro?

No not quite. Just got to chop up my Mom.

Whoa harsh.

She throw out your porn stash again?

Yeah.

*pick

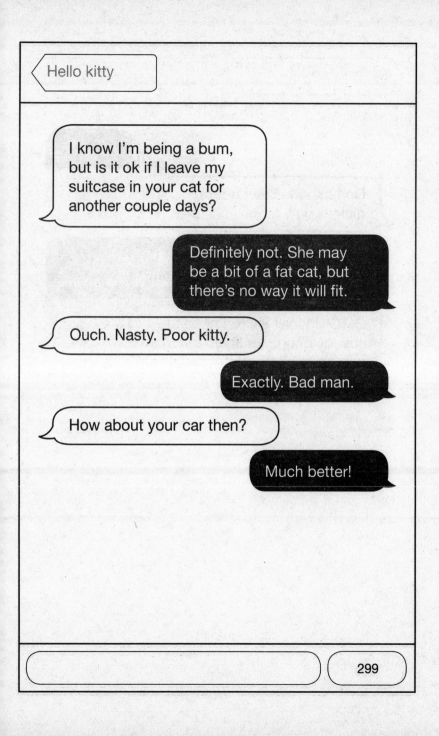

I know I'm being a bum, but is it ok if I leave my suitcase in your cat for another couple days?

Definitely not. She may be a bit of a fat cat, but there's no way it will fit.

Ouch. Nasty. Poor kitty.

Exactly. Bad man.

How about your car then?

Much better!

It could be worse. The vet said that she's got Star Wars. So they can definitely help.

OK. Utterly speechless.

I always knew your cat was Darth Grievous.

Stomach worms.

Dunno which is stranger, your phone or your cat.

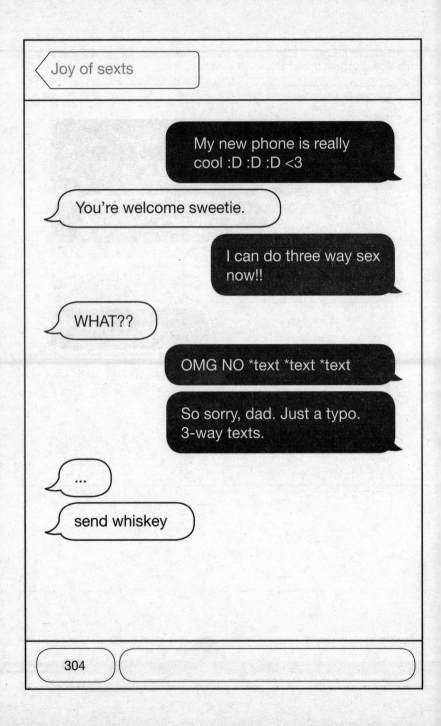

You all right?

Gah. Not really. Got into a shit-load of trouble at work. Gave this guy a really hard jacking off.

WTF????????

Oh great. No! Goddam phone. I gave this piece of shit a really hard telling off for being a total dick to Stace. A customer. Manager went ballistic.

FM. Shitty. Life.

Think I asshole go to the crow this evening?

I don't think you typed what you think you typed.

Princess Blade, Jim? I'm impressed!

*bride. *show. *should.

I need a neutron.

Yeah. You so do.

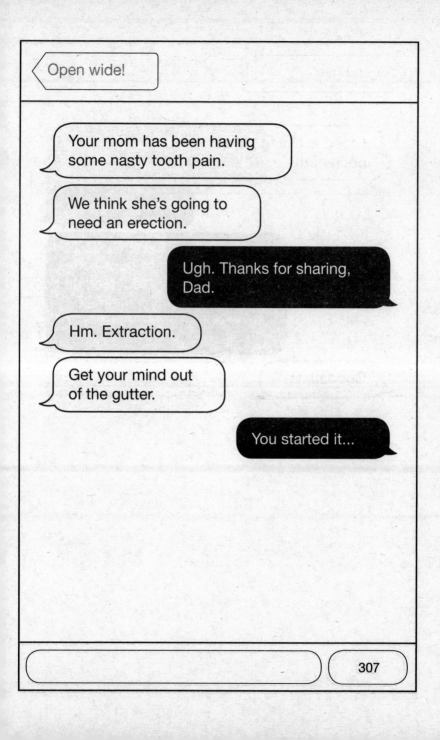

I aced it. Not to blow my poon horn.

BWAHAHAHA

Yeah. Don't want to blow your poon-horn, dude. You need ribs removed first, or you'll break your spine. Besides, NASTY.

Goddamnit.

It was nice. They made us feel whalecum.

NOT NICE!

*welcome

Why the hell is whale cum in your phone?

Oh God. I mean, why does your phone have that term in it?

Ah, dammit.

My thoughts exactly.

I'm just heading into the office orgy now.

WTF. Not orgy. RIGHT. Office right now.

LOL!!!

I'm calling your director!

I think she's bent over the photocopier...

You around at the weekend?

Maybe. I gotta clean up my dad's dick though.

AAA HORRIBLE

*DECK

Now I really wish I hadn't asked!!

Gngngngngngn

Where did you vanish too?

I left your coffee on Steve's dick

*desk

I am *NOT* drinking anything from Steve's dick

Lol prolly for the best

What about tomorrow?

Even worse. Gotta be up at six for a ten-hour shit at work

HOLY CHRIST!

That would be a truly arse-busting nightmare of a dump. Talk about a bog-rocking turd the size of a submarine!!

Sod that for a game of soldiers! The shift is bad enough!

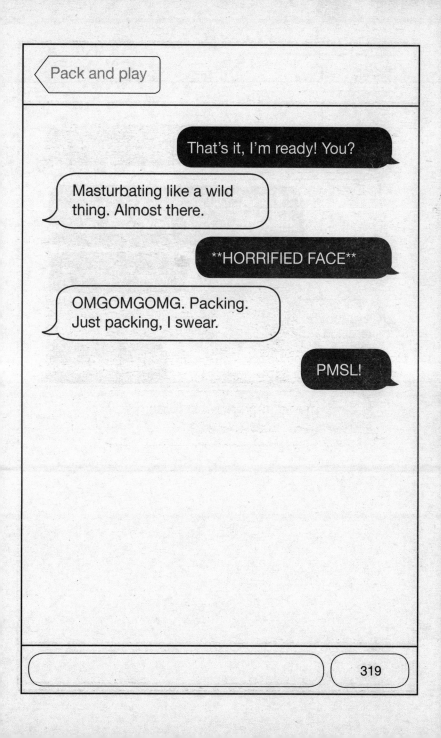